Tiger Laughs When You Push

Tiger Laughs When You Push

Ruth Lehrer

HEADMISTRESS PRESS

Copyright © 2016 by Ruth Lehrer.
All rights reserved.

ISBN-13: 978-0692604755
ISBN-10: 0692604758

This book may not be reproduced, in whole or in part, including illustrations, in any form (beyond that permitted by Sections 107 and 108 of the U.S. Copyright Law and except by reviewers for the public press), without written permission from the publishers.

Cover art © 2014 *Tiger Laughs* by Christina Schlesinger.
Cover & book design by Mary Meriam

PUBLISHER
Headmistress Press
60 Shipview Lane
Sequim, WA 98382
Telephone: 917-428-8312
Email: headmistresspress@gmail.com
Website: headmistresspress.blogspot.com

Contents

Wishing Ill on People	1
Animal Cracker	2
Sucking Lemon Pickle	3
Of being in that demoralized place ...	4
Losing Teeth	5
Foreign Imports	6
Molting	7
Détente	8
Falling	9
The meaning of blot	10
I don't believe in marriage	11
Chicken or Egg	12
Splinter the	13
Shopping Cart	14
Duck Smoke	16
The Progression of Nasties	17
Breakfast	18
No Love is Unconditional	19
Catherine	20
Infixes	21
City Sounds	22
March Heist	23
You Wolf You	24
Acknowledgments	25
About the Author	26

Wishing Ill on People

Really, it's not that general
Really, it's mostly specific
for a good reason
with a fine line
between vengeance and spite.
I don't wish they would die
No, really I want something
more drawn out
like a landscape
with lots of layers.
You think you're done
with the sheep
and then you see
the watching wolves.
Really, like that
but more painful.

Animal Cracker

Tiger laughs when you push
She already has dirt with her donut
and knows the cage is cardboard.
She's savvy on feeds of zoos and booze
She gets a kick
from slow prey
and a large coke with ice.
She sasses the tiger cha-cha
past catfish claws and spies in spice.
At night she snorts
when you try to tell her
the jungle
is dangerous.

Sucking Lemon Pickle

When I moved to the all-white school,
the not-white girl
taught me to suck Indian lemon pickle
straight from the jar.
Dragging pulpy fire-peel
across our adolescent tongues,
we sat on her high kitchen stools
swinging our naked toes,
licking the salty red chili pepper kick.

When I moved to the dirt poor mountains,
the Deaf woman
with the spiteful child and the running roaches on the floor,
picked me a wild strawberry
from her lawn.
And even though her garage was full of rotting trash
and a dead cat,
I ate it
and she gave me another.

Of being in that demoralized place and having things flying over your head, not understanding anything

I wait for the full glass
dirty jokes and pompom poems
laundry lists like small cities
in the palm of a hand.

My glass filling up
each liquid drop
every un-understood
every missed snide hiss
every flick of the hand
I pretend I get
but don't—
A drop into the unfull cup.

Up patience
Level up by one
embarrassment milliliter
One small foot or small mouth
kick myself up an ounce
I wait for years.

But each missed wit
each lost twitch
is a drop
towards up.

Losing Teeth

My mother sent me a napkin of rotted teeth.
Did she think they were sweet?
returning them, a donation of precious?
Or was it a clearing
of all that used to be me
from her pillows of mind.
Postage cut from matter gone canine.
There was no warning.
When I peeled open
ancient paper
to the baby decay within
I shuddered,
and let go.

Foreign Imports

Westchester Chinese food suffers
from white suburbia
a disease of distance
25 whole highway miles
from Queens
the land of red and spicy banquet halls
lotus seeds and sweet rice
8 treasures flipped on a golden platter.

I am bitter
when we settle for Yonkers dim sum
instead of crossing the bridge.
Even the Westchester waiters know
they are serving second rate.
They don't complain of foreign imports
when we open up the cake box.
They look at the red characters on the white box
and they heave big Chinese sighs.
Queens, they say,
Food from the homeland.

Molting

They found Grandma on the couch
beneath the swinging parrot cage.
Cold and hollow-boned
lightly covered in the sand of a bird's burial,
a green feather sticky on her shoulder.

The family fought over the parrot
as if it were polished silver from the old country,
which in a way it was
since her lilting Lithuanian
still squawked,
a bird's lifetime feeding on dying dialect
and old lady phone calls.

The son's inheritance feathered his finger in red,
gashed to the bone by the snapping Lithuanian beak,
so his wife relived Grandma's hardshelled hand,
opening sunflowers for the sad green head.

When the bird dropped dead
of time and tongue hunger,
the widowed wife wound the body in green plastic wrap
and murmured what she thought might sound
like Lithuanian prayer.

Détente

A military man
forty years
in the people's liberation
army, now he grows
a garden in a westchester suburb.
Fighting the chemo and
the foreign food
he speaks only chinese
and I only english.
We meet in gestural middle
to discuss his eggplants
qié zi – my one chinese word.
Tempting fate
he plants my two
new england garlics
and the next year
he has eight.

Falling

I shake out the tablecloth
from the terrace of Grandma's
Central Park West apartment.
No more fireworks
over the East river,
just crumbs of breakfasts gone.

My grandfather used to scoop out
the insides of English muffins
since that was where all bad calories lived.
But he'd been gone a dozen years,
the crumbs couldn't be his.

That's what I think of though, seeing
the tiny falling bodies flap
over black metal railing
to taxi tops below.

We peel fifty years of art
off soon-to-be condo walls.
Grand pianos humming goodbye
to Central Park living.

I shake out the tablecloth
from the apartment terrace.
A single silver spoon
falls eighteen floors
to hard concrete.

The meaning of blot

Eden squatted
menstrual blood paintings
which she hung
on the dorm wall
near the bathroom.
A Rorschach
blot on parents weekend.
Now she looks up
uteruses for a living
on Long Island.
I assume
she uses gloves and
she gave up art.

I email my uterus and ask
how is the weather up in heaven.
She texts back
blots of sun and beach.
Doctors
say to mourn her loss,
blot gone to
scissors and knives.
Male doctors
have no art in their past.
They think blot
means ghost
up and gone.

But somehow my grey gloves,
lost at a bus stop
on a rainy night,
haunt me more.

I don't believe in marriage

You think I'm a house
cat but really I'm a tigerfish
house built up on black claws
against orange seamarsh breasts.
I'm an invasive species.
A predator with a herring tail.
A monster under the seabed
floor. A feline crab
living in your bedroom sewer.

Chicken or Egg

My poet friend
sells handbags and purses and wishes
for chickens so much
they ooze out on the page and from her
eyes. Peeking out from syllables she asks
if an egg is sacrilege
when you eat it poached
on toast?
I say, no, of course
not, a poached egg is to a chicken
as a word is to a poem
and how many words do we
spend every day
between selling
handbags? and purses and wishes?
Untold.

Splinter the

Glass catalyst
like snow white the bad apple
they tell me bifocals are out of phase

Refracted between close and far
I'd rather see far
you can twist the neck of something close
but that thing far
you can see where it's heading before it gets there
Leopard scat or creature hair
Even with its neck broken I can't see me

Like a boat with a glass bottom
under water under time
I strain
like a carnivorous papercup-and-string phone

A jittering snow globe of brain
Bring back lines!
I want to see where
my brain is supposed to
flat up and dimension down

I drink soapy water
for the electrolytes

And I squint.

Shopping Cart

She's kind of an
adjectival person
so it was hard
to see her
like zucchini
shunned by the neighbors
locked doors
and bad breads
I went on a bad date
with her once.

I'm all for italics, she said
Me too, I said
although my typewriter
was stuck on B
It wasn't even electronic
I'm talking carbon
paper I'm talking mimeo
graph purple
You're dating yourself, she said,
like a price sticker
on the bottom of a bottle of beans.

Waylaid in the cereal aisle on dialup
corn flaking
cheerio walking
poptarting
oh the pop! oh the tart!
I lose her in piles of Post puffed rice.

Heartcracked, I need cereal lowjack
fruit GPS
to get out from under
the cheesy cheers.

My shopping cart
it has bad wheels
all kinked backwards
when actually
I was going straight.

Duck Smoke

For the first time
she had to knife a neck
off a duck cadaver
which then she left in hot
and wine over a night of cold
All she had was a sad cake box
to hold its duck wild in
But in morning
she hung it by colander
holes of air to speak
through day

I think in evening
it was all smoke
But I'm not sure.

The Progression of Nasties
or Hives and the Crumbly Language

My girlfriend says my father and I
are the same. Not only are we glass-half-empty
people, but the glass is leaking too.
But no matter, got to talk now,
got to ring up the other man
and say Hey, what's the deal? I mean
you got a degree and a long distance phone.
You got a high dose wacktacker and a needle
the length of my dick. Well, not my
dick but someone else with a dick. The length of.

I wrestled down your pig latin and now
you want me to stop by the window too.
Sorry, I'm waiting for the google earth of intestines
the touch screen of ovary thoughts
the audio book of digestion.

Mirror through half glass is pretty cloudy
but I will say,

Just looking at you
gives me hives.

Breakfast

Spatter pattern
is what we called
the crumbs in the toaster tray

Way too many now to see a pattern
they used to tell the future
like gluten tea leaves on a cloudy day

Now I burn a bagel
and no one even mentions the chance
of meeting a dark-eyed stranger
or that my lucky number is 9

We used to grind butter
left on greasy paper
Together we'd make shadow animals of butterfat
and spread rancid margarine rumors
Coddle the Egg
dialing 900 numbers
—Hello, this is Spanky —
before the pan gets too hot
Hot like a griddle or a cake
sex is lost by the time the timer
buzzes 9 minutes before 9.

No bagel no bialy
I predict I'll starve
for a piece of toast.

No Love is Unconditional

My neighbors killed their goats
but not on purpose
or so they say
It was like they knew the story
but weren't paying enough attention
to the plot
like the creepy postman
like the haunted shower
like the bloody casserole but
baked on a hand hacked wood fire

My neighbors painted only
the north wall of their house
Up on a ladder
with the phone on the ground just in case
Because that was the wall
on the road side
on the people side

Like a goat on the run
Like a ladder with a broken rung
I ring their phone and then
breathing heavy hearts
hang up.

Catherine

She was looking
for a hard edge
but I had hard too.
I had cheese blintzes,
she must have had
hot pastrami.
She thought I'd be backed up
against a wall
but I ordered tea
not coffee.
I said I'm bi
in such a butch way
that despite my hippie hair
and young hands
she had to respect,
along with the applesauce
and sour cream,
that I asked for both.

Blintzes are still on the menu board
but she is past pastrami
hardly hot
A machine breathing
for her hard edge.

Infixes

I asked her what it meant
and she wrote
un-fucking-believable

I saw her years later and
people were still asking me
and I still knew exactly
what she meant by *cohort*
and how you *compound a plural*

Afterwards she gave me her card
but only to make us paper
not blood

She was the kind to talk about
how you can't say *eggs* sandwich
or *nails* clipper
and how you create order from disorder

Oh now I've outed her
when I meant to be a kind of
secrets keeper
for forgotten tongues

But that's not important
she still resides
infixed between
amygdala and craw.

City Sounds

I knew a man who soundproofed
his Fenway apartment with egg
cartons. Was it heat? Was it art?
Glued up on the ceiling with egg white or poop
I didn't ask
He took me to the roof
and tried to kiss—an old egg carton pucker
But his old man sweater smelled
like bad egg and cat pee
and so I said no thanks
He was married
after a fashion
twice
He couldn't see well
after a fashion
once
Did he hear those city egg cartons scream?
I didn't ask.

March Heist

Winter time freezes spit on trees
and west river obituaries
snow crumble dustmud
on underside of leaves

What do you mean by that?
They ask me that a lot

You'd think I got paid in apples
like an orchard of teeth
but I have a defect of water
not blood
not metaphoric
but true as ice

Or maybe mud?
Send me a wind
through squirrel nests
words chewed beyond
what we would call words

Floating white is how I image it

I look for fast clear water
to let me draw a breath
but it runs into crystal
and carbon and walls that suck inward

Pretty perhaps but
almost as useful as
porcelain teeth for hunting
when you don't
go outside
for three months
and counting

You Wolf You

We named the bed Lola
and the stove Pristine
and played house until
we got landlocked with floods

What happened to those floods
I get frozen by the idea of water so great
and words so many I have to pick
the driest and most safe
where pencil draws behind
without ink or typeface
to screw up the depression
that comes after a water world

We cooked a cream soup
with ginger compote
singing in the back of our tongues
When we cut through dairy
with our teeth
You didn't even
need a knife

Grey eyes with red lines
Line red with eyes grey
You wolf you
I try to emulate you

Acknowledgments

Thanks to the editors of the following publications where these poems first appeared:

Blue Hour Magazine: "No Love is Unconditional"

Everyday Genius: "Wishing Ill on People" and "Duck Smoke"

Jubilat: "March Heist"

Oddball Magazine: "City Sounds"

Off the Coast: "Molting"

So To Speak: "The Meaning of Blot"

Trivia: Voices of Feminism: "Animal Cracker" and "I Don't Believe in Marriage"

Wordgathering: "Sucking Lemon Pickle"

Zig Zag Folios: "Infixes" and "A Progression of Nasties"

About the Author

Ruth Lehrer is a writer and sign language interpreter living in western Massachusetts. Her fiction and poetry have been published in journals such as *Jubilat, Trivia: Voices of Feminism, Zig Zag Folios,* and *Everyday Genius.* Find her at ruthlehrer.com

Headmistress Press Books

Lovely - Lesléa Newman
Teeth & Teeth - Robin Reagler
How Distant the City - Freesia McKee
Shopgirls - Marissa Higgins
Riddle - Diane Fortney
When She Woke She Was an Open Field - Hilary Brown
God With Us - Amy Lauren
A Crown of Violets - Renée Vivien tr. Samantha Pious
Fireworks in the Graveyard - Joy Ladin
Social Dance - Carolyn Boll
The Force of Gratitude - Janice Gould
Spine - Sarah Caulfield
Diatribe from the Library - Farrell Greenwald Brenner
Blind Girl Grunt - Constance Merritt
Acid and Tender - Jen Rouse
Beautiful Machinery - Wendy DeGroat
Odd Mercy - Gail Thomas
The Great Scissor Hunt - Jessica K. Hylton
A Bracelet of Honeybees - Lynn Strongin
Whirlwind @ Lesbos - Risa Denenberg
The Body's Alphabet - Ann Tweedy
First name Barbie last name Doll - Maureen Bocka
Heaven to Me - Abe Louise Young
Sticky - Carter Steinmann
Tiger Laughs When You Push - Ruth Lehrer
Night Ringing - Laura Foley
Paper Cranes - Dinah Dietrich
On Loving a Saudi Girl - Carina Yun
The Burn Poems - Lynn Strongin
I Carry My Mother - Lesléa Newman
Distant Music - Joan Annsfire
The Awful Suicidal Swans - Flower Conroy
Joy Street - Laura Foley
Chiaroscuro Kisses - G.L. Morrison
The Lillian Trilogy - Mary Meriam
Lady of the Moon - Amy Lowell, Lillian Faderman, Mary Meriam
Irresistible Sonnets - ed. Mary Meriam
Lavender Review - ed. Mary Meriam

www.ingramcontent.com/pod-product-compliance
Lightning Source LLC
Chambersburg PA
CBHW070047070426
42449CB00012BA/3181